W. PARKER SEAMENS OUTFITTING

ERG 833

INDUSTRIAL
STEAM

IN THE '50S & '60S

ERIC SAWFORD

First published in 2004 by
Sutton Publishing Limited · Phoenix Mill
Thrupp · Stroud · Gloucestershire · GL5 2BU

Front endpaper: Steam locomotives that worked on a public highway were required to have protection over work parts. This can be seen on Andrew Barclay No. 2239 of 1947, pictured at Aberdeen. 12.8.55

Back endpaper: During the early fifties three locomotives could usually be found at work during the season at the British Sugar Corporation, Peterborough. Among these was Avonside No. 1945 of 1926.
4.12.54

British Library Cataloguing in Publication Data
A catalogue record for this book is available from the British Library.

ISBN 0-7509-3646-0

Typeset in 10/12 pt Palatino.
Typesetting and origination by
Sutton Publishing Limited.
Printed and bound in England by
J.H. Haynes & Co. Ltd, Sparkford.

Contents

Introduction

Many, but fortunately not all, railway enthusiasts paid little attention to industrial locomotives during the 1950s as their main concern was British Railways motive power. At this time there was still a vast number of 'industrials' quietly going about their business. They ranged from those employed on the extensive rail systems of ports and collieries to the diminutive narrow-gauge engines working in the slate quarries of North Wales, where their presence was often only betrayed by a wisp of steam high in the mountains. By the 1960s things were changing rapidly on the main railway system as steam was replaced at an ever-increasing rate. Some steam enthusiasts turned their attention to the industrial lines while others, as steam finished, gave up their interest in railways altogether.

In my case I was always interested in both British Railways locomotives *and* industrial railway engines. Permission to visit private installations to take photographs was usually readily granted by companies who operated industrial steam. In many cases they were intrigued by the fact that someone was interested in their locomotives: after all, many had been in service for over forty years and were an everyday sight to them. Requests to move an engine to enable a good picture to be taken were, in the majority of cases, readily granted. It was of course always important to bear in mind that these were working railways and everyone had a job to do.

For those with an interest in narrow-gauge railways North Wales was a great attraction. I visited the Penrhyn system at Bethesda on several occasions. Not only did it operate railways on various levels, it also had its own main line for transporting slate to the port. This was usually operated by three engines, two of which, *Blanche* and *Linda*, were later to go to the Ffestiniog railway, where they proved invaluable additions to their motive power. Many of the engines at Penrhyn were built by Hunslets of Leeds. There were a few others built by different companies that were purchased from various private companies over the years. These included two sturdy Andrew Barclays that came from the Durham Water Board. For many years a line of derelict engines stood at Bethesda, used only as a source of spare parts (although the weather had taken its toll). Few, including me, thought that they would ever run again. Fortunately, this was not the case as in time they were all purchased for preservation. In the late 1800s the local company De Winton of Caernarvon supplied vertical boiler locomotives to the Penrhyn and several other slate quarries, and one of these was to be found among the derelicts. These engines provided no protection for the driver,

(Opposite, top) Manning Wardle no. 1123 *Kettering Furnaces No. 6* of 1889 receives attention from its driver. The engine is coupled to one of the narrow-gauge wagons used on this system. All three of the Manning Wardles here were in use at the time of my visit, together with a veteran Black Hawthorn 0–4–0ST.   11.11.55

(Opposite, bottom) Over the years slate quarries built up large tips of waste slate, one of which can be seen on the right here. The ground is also littered with broken pieces. Built by Andrew Barclay in 1931, 0–4–0WT no. 1991 *Gegin* was supplied new to the Durham Water Board, being sold on to the Penrhyn slate quarries as reservoir construction came to an end. In total, the Penrhyn slate quarries purchased five engines from the Durham Water Board between 1934 and 1938, including *Gegin*. One of the others was also built by Andrew Barclay, with two built by Avonside and are by Kerr Stuart.   25.6.62

Hunslet no. 317 *Lilian* of 1883 was supplied new to the Penrhyn, where it was known as one of the Port class engines. It was built without a cab. Two Hunslets were purchased in 1883 to supplement the existing fleet of De Winton vertical boiler locomotives.
25.6.62

which was not a problem in the summer months but in winter it was a very different matter. Heavy rain, low cloud and icy winds would have made life very difficult indeed for the enginemen, especially on the higher levels.

Not far from Penrhyn was the Dinorwic system at Llanberis, where there was an extensive network of galleries cut into the mountainside. Motive power here was principally supplied by Hunslet designs. The Dinorwic also operated its own main line for transporting slates to Port Dinorwic where it was loaded on to rail or ship. Three interesting locomotives, all built by Hunslets, were the motive power for this line. They were sizeable 0–6–0Ts, the enginemen in this case having the luxury of a complete cab. When the line closed all three engines spent some time in sidings at Llanberis before being sold for scrap. This line was unusual in that it was 4ft gauge.

Narrow-gauge lines were also to be found at other locations. The Crown Portland Cement Company at Southam in Warwickshire, for example, operated several small Pecketts, all named after geological time periods. This was a fascinating railway, where comparatively small locomotives busied themselves moving loaded hopper wagons. One of the most extensive narrow-gauge systems was to be found at Sittingbourne and was operated by Bowaters United Kingdom Pulp & Paper Mills Ltd. The locomotives here were mostly fitted with unattractive spark arresters which did little to improve their appearance but reduced the risk of fire. The same company also operated a standard-gauge line on the docks. One of the engines here was a P class 0–6–0T of South Eastern & Chatham Railway origin, which carried the name *Pioneer II*. It was taken into British Railways stock and became no. 31178.

Some of the Bowaters' locomotives carried improvised shutters to offer protection to enginemen, this one looks suspiciously like a domestic window! The outside cylinder 0–6–2Ts were capable of handling heavy loads, and here Bagnall *Alpha* no. 2472 of 1932 heads a loaded train. 10.7.67

Late afternoon and the Samuel Williams' engines were arriving back on shed. No. 4 Manning Wardle no. 641/1877 was not supplied new to the company, arriving in 1889 via the South Wales dealer C.D. Phillips. When the company changed over to diesel power they retained no. 4 for preservation, as it was the oldest survivor. This was a very different attitude to many companies, who were only too pleased to see the last steam engine go. 24.5.56

During the 1950s Northamptonshire was still very much involved with ironstone production. One narrow-gauge system operating an extensive network of lines for the transportation of iron ore was to be found at Kettering, operated by the Kettering Iron & Coal Company. Principal motive power was three 0–6–0Ts built by Manning Wardle of Leeds. Two were supplied new and the third came from a contractor. There were also two veteran 0–4–0Ts built by Black Hawthorn, which were principally used on shunting and back-up work. These had only a spectacle plate and no doubt were unpopular as they provided little protection for the driver in inclement weather. A fairly extensive works nearby was operated until 1959 to deal with the iron ore. In this case it was standard gauge, although at least one of the locomotives had dual buffers.

During the 1950s Wellingborough was another interesting location with a stud of locomotives and a works nearby. One of the engines still to be found there in the mid-fifties was built way back in 1876 by Hudswell, Clarke & Rogers. It was especially interesting as it had been subject to considerable rebuilding over the years. In the area around Wellingborough there were a number of rail systems used for the transportation of iron ore. One, which was incorporated into the giant Stewart & Lloyds Minerals Group, consisted of a one-metre-gauge line operating three Pecketts, two of which were built in the 1940s. The South Durham Iron & Steel Company had iron ore workings at Irchester and Storefield. Its working stock included no. 4, an 0–4–0ST built by Manning Wardle in 1912 and rebuilt by Ridley Shaw in 1939. Nearby was a line of derelicts, most of which had been robbed for spares. The most interesting engine in the line-up was Peckett 0–4–0ST no. 1258 of 1912, *Rothwell*, which still had its early pattern safety valves.

During the 1950s iron ore quarries were still to be found in Oxfordshire and Lincolnshire. Much of the ore was transported to other parts of the country by rail. Meanwhile in Northamptonshire ironworks were still active at Wellingborough and Kettering, and at the massive complex at Corby. The ironworks at Islip had closed in 1943, although the quarry lines remained active until 1952. Not far away was the Cranford Ironstone Co. Ltd, a quarry whose iron ore was transported by way of Kettering and the Midland main line. Nearby was a 2ft system which operated a small Bagnall 0–4–0ST, no. 2090 *Pixie* of 1919. Northamptonshire had had numerous rail systems over the years but by the 1950s some had been closed for a considerable time. Sadly they have all now become part of our history.

Sugar beet is an important farming crop and has been for many years, with large processing factories handling the crop during the autumn and winter period. Several such factories were rail-linked and required motive power. Today things have changed. Road transport is used, and there are fewer processing plants. One extensive rail system was to be found at Wissington in Norfolk, where the locomotives not only worked at the factory itself but also transported incoming supplies from a network of fields. I only made one visit to this rail system, but it was during the closed season when all the engines were standing idle in the yard, as they did for much of the spring and summer. Two Manning Wardle 0–6–0STs built in 1901 and 1921 were present, together with a Hudswell Clarke 0–4–0ST, no. 533 of 1899. The lines closed in 1957 and most of the track, except in the vicinity of the factory, was soon lifted.

Power stations, gasworks, the Coal Board and a great many other companies operated their own rail systems. Some had just one or two engines, while others had extensive fleets.

(Opposite, top) You could hardly miss this Hawthorn, Leslie & Co. Ltd engine, no. 18, at Stewart & Lloyds of Corby. The locomotive, in vivid yellow livery, had warning markings on the buffer beam. Built as works no. 3896 in 1936, it was one of several Hawthorns supplied new in the 1930s.   12.11.55

(Opposite, bottom) Only a comparatively small number of British Railways industrial locomotives found their way into private ownership over the years. *Pioneer II*, seen here at Bowaters' Ridham Dock, was built by the SECR in 1910 at their Ashford Works and eventually carried the BR number 31178. The original *Pioneer* was a Manning Wardle engine, built in 1885 and scrapped in 1954.   10.7.67

The majority were cooperative regarding visits, but some were difficult to get to (unless you had your own transport) owing to their isolated locations.

Considering the vast number of industrial locomotives in use at one time, it is surprising that more were not purchased from British Railways, and before that from the 'big four' after grouping. Most of the engines that in later years were eventually to find their way into private ownership belonged to the National Coal Board and London Transport, and many of them were ex-Western Region pannier tanks.

The industrial locomotives that were given a new lease of life included a few surprises. The National Coal Board purchased several examples from the smaller Welsh companies that became part of the Great Western, and these were to find themselves working at collieries in County Durham. Among them were engines that at one time had been owned by the Alexandra Dock, Cardiff, Barry and Taff Vale railways. The Coal Board also had examples from the North Staffs Railway at Walkden in Manchester and two ex-North Eastern locomotives that worked in County Durham.

Ex-main line railway locomotives could be found in unexpected places. Thomas E. Gray of Burton Latimer in Northamptonshire, for example, purchased Sentinel no. 12 from the Great Eastern, an engine that was very similar to those already being used on the Eastern Region of British Railways. The massive Corby steelworks had in its extensive fleet an ex-Caledonian Railway 0–4–0ST, built in 1902. These engines were of a type widely known as 'Pugs'. Formerly LMS no. 16037, it had arrived at Stewart & Lloyds from Cadzow Colliery in 1945 and became S&L no. 27. It stood in a run-down state in the locomotive shed for some time before being scrapped.

Many of the countless industrial locomotives that once worked in the British Isles were probably never photographed, as enthusiasts were more interested in the more glamorous passenger engines. Shunting was once a familiar sight at countless yards on British Railways, the work often continuing through the night as well, but few enthusiasts bothered to photograph the industrial engines that did this work at so many locations. Now they are part of our railway history.

1. Four-Coupled – Standard Gauge

Many private rail systems had track layouts that included tight curves, thus requiring short-wheelbase locomotives to work on them, and the four-coupled wheel arrangement was ideal. One problem that could arise under certain circumstances was buffer locking. Hence locomotives were often fitted with 'dumb buffers' consisting of wooden blocks, usually with a metal face.

The working day of an industrial engine varied greatly. Those at gas works and power stations handled incoming supplies and return empties, and such roles could involve periods of inactivity. Locomotives at steel works, collieries and busy dock areas usually had a much more intensive working pattern. During the 1950s and 1960s there were industrial engines were to be found at countless different locations. Some companies had just a single engine, and hired a replacement in the event of a major breakdown or when maintenance work was required. Others had a stand-by engine. At the other end of the scale were the big companies with fleets of engines: for example, the Manchester Ship Canal had around eighty engines at one time.

Often these private rail systems had some parts that required short-wheelbase engines, while the majority of work was in the hands of their larger cousins of six-coupled designs, so the companies concerned had a variety of engines – good for enthusiasts!

Andrew Barclay no. 2168 of 1943, *Edmundsons*, at Little Barford power station. Short-wheelbase locomotives like this sturdy 0–4–0ST were essential here because of the tight curves, as can be seen on the right of this picture. 2/02 The electricity generating station at Little Barford was owned by the Edmundson Electricity Corporation until 1949, when it was taken over by the Central Electricity Generating Board.   28.9.69

Two steam locomotives were to be found at Little Barford Power Station, both built by Andrew Barclay and supplied new. *Edmundsons* works no. 2168, built in 1943, was the youngest. It was named after the owners Edmundsons Electricity Corporation Ltd until 1948 when it became part of the Central Electricity Generating Board.   7.4.66

Note the short and well-proportioned wheelbase, the handbrake outside the cab and the large works plate. Incoming coal supplies to Little Barford power station were received via the East Coast main line. Pictures of *Edmundsons* have been selected as they provide much interesting detail for railway modellers.   7.4.66

In 1954 Andrew Barclay supplied two new 0–4–0STs to the Central Electricity Generating Board at Goldington power station, Bedford. No. 2354 *Richard Trevithick*, built in 1954, carried the number ED 10.   28.9.69

Dwarfed by a British Railways standard iron ore wagon, locomotive no. 8, Yorkshire Engine Company no. 784 of 1902, is seen here on shunting duties at the Charwelton ironstone quarries, which were owned by the Park Gate Iron & Steel Company. This immaculate engine was a credit to its driver – even the brass works plate had been polished. It had a short wheelbase, presumably for use on the tight curves at Park Gate Ironworks in Rotherham where it had worked previously. It was supplied new to Rotherham, moving to Charwelton in 1952.   24.11.54

The oldest engine working at the South Durham Steel & Iron Company at Irchester in 1967 was Manning Wardle *No. 14*, built as works number 1795 in 1912 and rebuilt in 1936 by Ridley Shaw. It came from the Wensley Lime Company of Preston-under-Scar in Yorkshire in 1957. This company was a subsidiary of the South Durham. Originally *No. 14* also worked at John Lysaght in Scunthorpe, being supplied by a Sheffield dealer.   16.3.67

There was an unforgettable moment when *No. 14* became derailed as it ran back to the depot. There was a loud bang and this is how it ended up. Problems such as this were not uncommon; already staff had brought along a trolley and were preparing to jack the engine back on to the track.

3.8.67

This view of the Sentinel shows the opposite side to the chain drive. This locomotive worked at Coldhams Lane Sidings in Cambridge, where it was used to shunt wagons through the Tippler until rail traffic ceased here in 1969.　　9.5.55

(*Opposite, top*) This unusual Sentinel 4WTG was built as works no. 8024 in 1929 and was supplied new to the Cambridge University & Town Gas-Light Company, which became part of the Eastern Gas Board in 1949.

(*Opposite, bottom*) Clearly visible are the chain drive and the famous Sentinel works plate, identical to those fitted on the steam wagons produced in large numbers by this company.　　9.5.55

Avonside no. 1875 of 1921 pictured at the Rugby Cement Company's Barrington Works. It was used as a stand-by engine at this time but was in excellent external condition in smart green livery. 13.4.69

Bowaters had two locomotives for shunting at Ridham Dock. Bagnall 0–4–0ST *Jubilee*, built in 1936 as works no. 2542, was one. The other was a former SECRP class 0–6–0T built in 1910 and named *Pioneer* II. 10.7.67

Cement works by the very nature of their activities were dusty places. Despite this, *Langar* Pecket no. 1703 of 1926 was kept in good external condition at Associated Portland Cement Manufacturers' Barnston Cement Works.

4.6.66

Many ironstone lines were at one time to be found in Northamptonshire. The South Durham Steel & Iron Company Ltd had operations at Irchester and Storefield. No. 9, Andrew Barclay works number 2323 of 1952, was to be found at Irchester.   26.12.65

Considerable periods of time elapsed at some quarries before the next load of ironstone was ready and if you were lucky you could catch locomotives during these periods, as here. *No. 17*, Hawthorn Leslie no. 3946 of 1927, was supplied new to the Irchester Company, which later became part of the South Durham Steel & Iron Company.   6.5.65

Movement of the engines used at ironstone quarries was by no means unusual. *No. 9* had fairly recently moved to the South Durham Company at Irchester when this picture was taken. It is a typical example of the postwar Andrew Barclay design. Built in 1952 as no. 2323, this engine was rather unusual in that it was fitted with dumb buffers. Two identical locomotives were in use at Irchester, *No. 9* and *No. 7*, works no. 2324, also built by Barclays in 1952.   16.3.67

Two Hawthorn Leslie 0–4–0STs were supplied new to Irchester Quarries, *No. 17* (works no. 3946) in 1937, the other a year earlier. Here *No. 17* is taking on water from a rather small diameter hose. 16.3.67

Shanks & McEwans Corby 0–4–0ST *Glendon* was built by Hudswell Clarke as works no. 1285 in 1917. It was sold to the company in 1953 by Glendon East Ironstone Quarries, which had traded as the Stanton Ironworks Company until 1950. 12.11 55

Two Andrew Barclay 0–4–0STs were at work on the tight curves at Stewart & Lloyds Corby Steelworks. This is *No. 1*, no. 762 of 1895, which came from Clydesdale Works in 1933 where it had carried the name *Clydesdale 6*. 12.11.55

Locomotives owned by Stewart & Lloyds were, on occasions, moved to various sites within the group to cover shortages. No. 36 *Isham*, built by Hunslets of Leeds in 1902 as works no. 791, had originally come from a quarry of the same name, and most of its working life was spent at Wellingborough Ironworks. When this picture was taken at Corby its working days were already over. 12.11.55

At first glance Stewart & Lloyds Corby *No. 26* hardly looks its age, but it was in fact built in 1890 as works no. 678, making it sixty-five years old. It was purchased in April 1945 from the Bent Colliery Company at Cadzow Hamilton.
12.11.55

(Opposite, top) Port of Par Ltd had two of these cut-down Bagnall 0–4–0STs, both of which were supplied new. No. 3058 *Alfred* was just three years old when this picture was taken, being built at Stafford in 1953. Low bridges on the line required the use of locomotives of this type.
6.9.56

(Opposite, bottom) The first of the two Bagnall 0–4–0STs supplied to the Port of Par was this one, works no. 2572 built in 1937. Before the arrival of the second engine in 1953, its workload had been shared with a Sentinel built in 1927. At the time of my visit the Sentinel was out of use and covered with a tarpaulin.
6.9.56

Among the
locomotives to
arrive at Samuel
Williams in 1940
was this Andrew
Barclay 0–4–0ST,
no. 1129 of 1907. Its
previous owner was
the Pumpherston
Oil Company in
Midlothian. 24.5.56

Most of the locomotives at Samuel Williams were 0–6–0STs. No. 14 *Maryhill* was one of the exceptions. Built by Peckett & Sons of Bristol in 1923 as works no. 1607, it was rebuilt by Sheppard of Bridgend in 1939 and sold the same year to Samuel Williams. Note the huge dockside cranes in the background.   24.5.56

(Opposite) Two Peckett 0–4–0STs were to be found at Southern Wharves Ltd of Dibles Wharf, Northam, Southampton. Works no. 2128 of 1952 *(above)* was supplied new while Peckett no. 1638 of 1923 *Bristol*, was supplied via Pecketts, having previously been in the ownership of the Barnsley Gas Company, which bought it new. It is seen here *(below)* in steam during a quiet period.   9.11.55

The Scottish Gas Board's Granton Works in Edinburgh operated two rail systems, one of standard gauge and the other 2ft 6in. Andrew Barclay 0–4–0STs provided the motive power in steam days, fitted with dumb buffers indicating tight curves on the tracks. *(Above)* No. 1890 was built at Kilmarnock in 1926. *(Below)* No. 1967 of 1935, in a work-stained condition, is busy shunting in the yard. Note the rivets round the edge of the smokebox door.   22.8.55

Years of exposure to the elements had taken their toll on no. 5, Sentinel no. 5735 of 1926, which was supplied new to Samuel Williams at Dagenham. Rust has already eaten its way through the metalwork. It had been left standing in a siding with two derelict Manning Wardle 0–6–0STs, nos 8 and 9. In January 1957 all three were sent to Cohens of Canning Town for scrap. 24.5.56

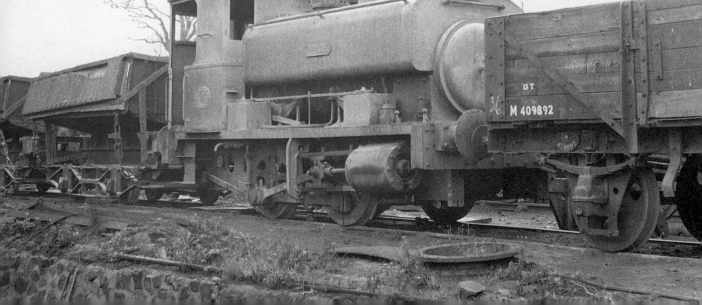

Resplendent in its lined green livery, Peckett no. 1375 of 1914 stands outside the single road shed of the Chapel Tramway Company, Southampton. At one time two locomotives were to be found here. 9.11.55

(Opposite, top) Hawthorn Leslie built this sturdy 0–4–0ST no. 3813 *Wellingborough No. 3* in 1935. It was one of the few locomotives supplied new to Wellingborough Ironworks. The engine is seen here engaged on shunting wagons of scrap metal. 11.11.55

(Opposite, bottom) Dumped with an assortment of wagons at Wellingborough Ironworks, this is Andrew Barclay no. 1645 *Foch*, built in 1919. Judging by its appearance, the locomotive had not worked for some time. It had in fact arrived from Stewart & Lloyds at Bilston eight months before this picture was taken. 11.11.55

(Overleaf) The Zephyr driver had taken a chance by parking on the railway lines at Aberdeen docks. Andrew Barclay 0–4–0ST no. 2239 of 1947 was the youngest of three owned by the Scottish Gas Board and employed at Aberdeen Gas Works. It is fitted with side-sheets over the moving parts for working through the streets. 24.8.55

By far the most interesting locomotive to be found at the Scottish Gas Board Aberdeen Gas Works was the Black, Hawthorn & Company Ltd 0–4–0ST no. 912 *City of Aberdeen*, built in 1887. Already sixty-eight years old when this picture was taken it was still in daily use in the works area. It was fitted with supports allowing plates to cover the moving parts when it was working in public places. These were removed when it was employed as works yard shunter. Note also the shaped dome fitted to this engine.   24.8.55

(Opposite, above and below) The removal and disposal of slag was an important job at Wellingborough Ironworks as it was elsewhere. Andrew Barclay no. 8, built as no. 2136 of 1941, was supplied new. It is seen here with a typical tipping slag wagon. The sign on the left reads 'Danger level crossing, pedestrians must not stand on this crossing', hardly to be recommended with a succession of trains passing.   11.11.55

Rather strange names could often be found on industrial locomotives. *The Broke,* Andrew Barclay no. 1592 of 1918, had not worked for some time when this picture was taken at Wellingborough Ironworks.   11.11.55

Holwell No. 19 Andrew Barclay no. 1826 of 1924, shunting wagons at Wellingborough Ironworks on a grey, dismal day. On the left is one of the slag disposal wagons used on site.   11.11.55

Industrial steam locomotives were few and far between in Norfolk, where the British Sugar Corporation was the principal operator. This early Hudswell Clarke 0–4–0ST was built in 1899 as works no. 533, and was purchased from McAlpine in 1925. It had not been in use for some time when this picture was taken and was scrapped in 1958.   8.5.54

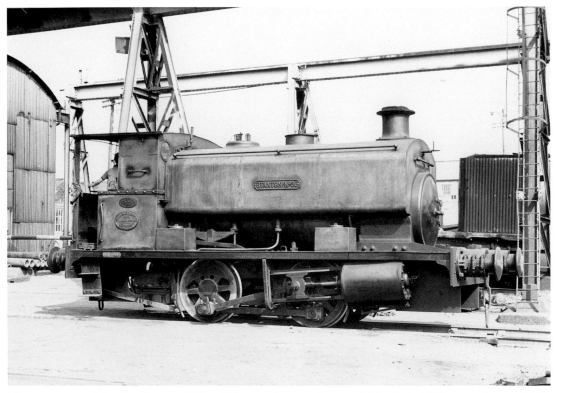

The youngest of the Barclays at Holwell Ironworks was *Stanton 36*, built in 1937 as works no. 2042. Work for the engines varied depending on traffic, but two or three were normally in use.   4.6.66

Stanton & Staveley Ltd had six locomotives at the Holwell Ironworks near Melton Mowbray in Leicestershire. Four were Andrew Barclays, including *Holwell 18*, no. 1791 of 1923. 4.6.66

(*Opposite, top*) Wear and tear was certainly showing on the chimney of *Holwell 18* at Holwell Ironworks. Damage to the cylinder cover is also evident. This engine was built in 1923 and is typical of the Barclays of the period. 4.6.66

(*Opposite, bottom*) Andrew Barclay no. 1047 of 1905 came to the South Durham Steel & Iron Company in 1922 from the Cargo Fleet Iron Company in Middlesbrough. It worked at both Irchester and Storefield, and is seen here near the latter. It carried a plate reading 'No. 11' on the cabside. In 1926 this engine was purchased by Irchester Ironstone Quarries and in 1949 the engine was rebuilt at Irchester. 16.3.67

(*Overleaf*) Time had run out for the sturdy 0-4-OST built in 1902 for the Caledonian Railway, later to become LMS No. 16037. It was to end its working days at Stewart & Lloyds Corby as No. 27. It was in a sorry state when towed out of the shed to be photographed. 14.11.55

Within Stewart & Lloyds' huge Corby complex the disposal of waste was the responsibility of Shanks & McEwan Ltd who operated their own locomotives. The Avonside Engine Company built no. 10 *Rosehall* at Bristol in 1901 as works no. 1435. It was at a Lancashire colliery until January 1944, when it arrived at Corby. The engine was nearing the end of its working days, and was scrapped two years after this picture was taken.   12.11.55

This veteran Andrew Barclay, works no. 306, was built in 1888. Although it was lying out of use when this picture was taken it had previously worked within the giant Stewart & Lloyds complex in the ownership of Shanks & McEwan.   12.11.55

Andrew Barclay 0–4–0STs were popular at Wellingborough Ironworks. *Holwell No. 19* was built by Barclay in 1924 as works no. 1826. It came to Wellingborough in 1943 from Stanton Ironworks. 11.11.55

Industrial locomotives at various ironstone quarries moved around quite frequently. *Holwell No. 30* had not long been at the South Durham Steel & Iron Company's Irchester site when this picture was taken. It was built by Hawthorn Leslie as works no. 3892 in 1936. 26.12.65

This veteran Hudswell Clarke & Rogers 0–4–0ST had not worked for a considerable period. Built in 1876 as works no. 180, it was rebuilt by Hudswell Clarke in 1920. It worked in several quarries in Northamptonshire before going to the ironworks and was officially withdrawn in 1958. It is seen here in company with Andrew Barclay *The Broke*.   11.11.55

(Opposite, top) The crew of this Kettering Ironworks engine were amazed to see someone photographing their Lingford Gardiner taking on water on a grey wet November day. Four standard-gauge engines were to be found at the ironworks in the mid-1950s. Time was running out, as the furnaces here ceased production in 1959.   11.11.55

(Opposite, bottom) Interesting locomotives were frequently found where you least expected them. This neat 0–4–0ST, *Kettering Furnaces No. 14*, was built by Lingford Gardiner in 1931 and arrived at Kettering via the company dismantling the builder's works. The standard-gauge engines at the ironworks were fitted with two sets of buffers, the lower set being used for narrow-gauge wagons.   11.11.55

This Andrew Barclay, works no. 1065 *Kettering No. 10*, at Kettering Ironworks was built in 1906, and rebuilt in 1941. It is seen here surrounded by steam and smoke on a dismal November day. As with the other standard-gauge engines, it had a double set of buffers.   11.11.55

(Opposite, top) Andrew Barclay *Major*, works no. 1363 of 1914, had moved around during its working life. Supplied new to the Seaton Carew Iron Company, it moved to the West Hartlepool Works of the South Durham Steel & Iron Company in 1928, remaining there until November 1957 when it moved to Irchester. It must have done little work as by 1965 it was among the derelicts.   26.12.65

(Opposite, bottom) Another of the derelict engines at Irchester was Hawthorn Leslie 0–4–0ST no. 3892, built in 1936. Surprisingly, it still had its works plate on the cabside. Most of the locomotives here arrived from other locations.
                                                                                                                26.12.65

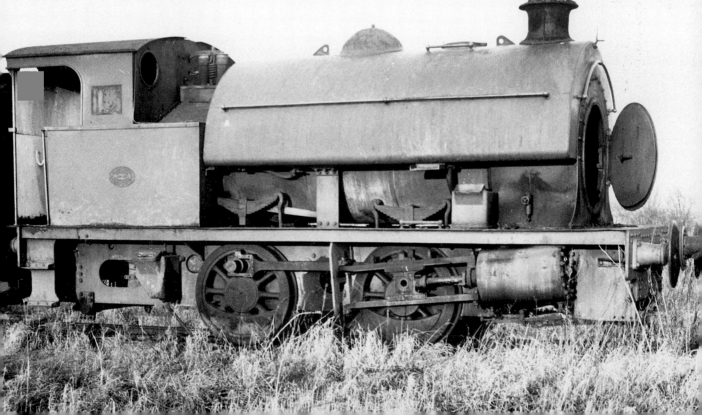

One thing about this engine that immediately catches the eye is the large dome and Salter safety valves, together with what remained of a makeshift chimney. Years of exposure had taken their toll on *Rothwell* by the time this photograph was taken.   30.1.66

(Opposite, top) It was by no means unusual to find industrial locomotives dumped in sidings and left to the elements once their working days were over. Occasionally they were robbed of parts to keep other engines in service. The South Durham Steel & Iron Company had several engines in this condition at Irchester. This is Andrew Barclay *1918*, works no. 1609 of that same year.   26.12.65

(Opposite, bottom) The Peckett *Rothwell*, works no. 1258 of 1912, was supplied new to Glendon North Ironstone Quarries before being sold on to the South Durham Steel & Iron Company at Irchester. The engine was named after a small Northamptonshire town in the ironstone area.   26.12.65

Thomas. E. Gray of Burton Latimer operated two Sentinels of this design, both of them built in 1946. No. 9369 *Musketeer* of 1946 originally worked for Williams & Williams Ltd of Hooton. The other engine, no. 9365, *Belvedere*, worked for W. Cory & Son of Rochester.   30.3.67

(Opposite, top) This Sentinel, works no. 6515 of 1926, started its working life on the Great Western Railway carrying the number 12 but it soon ended up back at the company's works. In due course it was sold to Thomas E. Gray Isebrook Quarry, Burton Latimer, where it became no. 2 *Isebrook*. It remained in service there until two new Sentinels were purchased. For many years it stood out of use and eventually it was purchased for preservation.   30.3.67

(Opposite, bottom) This National Coal Board Opencast Executive Hudswell Clarke 0–4–0ST, works no. 1727 of 1941, was used at Crigglestone in Yorkshire. The engine carries a plate reading *No. 1* on the cab and a nameplate *R. O. F. IS.* 20.3.66

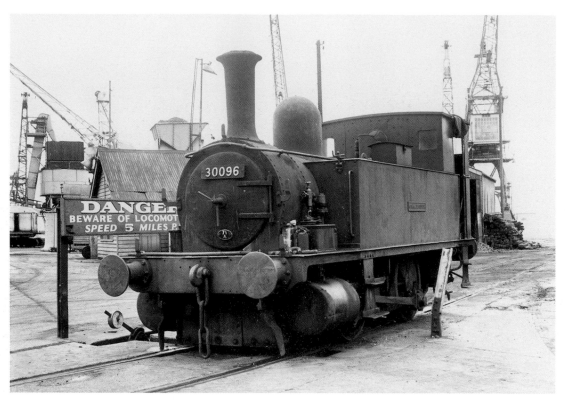

Still carrying its British Railways front numberplate and Eastleigh shed plate, this is B4 class no. 30096. Built by the LSWR in 1893, in its earlier working days it carried the name *Normandy*, but this was removed prior to BR ownership. When this picture was taken it had been renamed *Corrall Queen* and was owned by Corralls Fuel Distribution Ltd of Dibbles Wharf, Northam.   12.3.67

Corralls also owned a second locomotive, which was much younger than the B4. Robert Stephenson & Hawthorn built this 0–4–0ST no. 7544 in 1949. It carried the name *Bonnie Prince Charlie* and was lying out of use in a siding.   12.3.67

Hudswell Clarke no. 6 *Gwen*, works no. 1662, was supplied new to the Oxfordshire Ironstone Company in 1936. It is seen here banking a load of tipping ironstone wagons.   24.11.54

Oxfordshire Ironstone Company operated a considerable number of locomotives. Many were supplied new to the company although a few were brought in from elsewhere. 0–4–0ST *Newlay*, Hunslet no. 1292 of 1917, was one of these, being purchased from the Steel Company of Wales in 1951.   24.11.54

Exeter gas works operated two locomotives, both built by Peckett's of Bristol in the 1940s. No. 2074, seen here, was constructed in 1946. Normally only one engine would be in use each day.   4.9.56

(Opposite, top) A 26-ton iron ore tipping wagon of British Railways stock dwarfs this Manning Wardle engine, works no. 1795 built in 1912. This was a regular engine on the South Durham Steel & Iron Company's complex at Irchester.   30.8.67

(Opposite, bottom) Enterprise, a veteran 0–4–0ST, was built by Bagnalls of Stafford in 1907 as works no. 1739. It is seen here at the South Durham's Storefield shed. Much of the engine's life before the 1940s was spent in colliery ownership.
                                                                                                                       30.8.67

William Doxford & Sons of the Pallion shipyard in Sunderland operated a number of crane tanks. *Millfield*, was built by Robert Stephenson & Hawthorns as works no. 7070 and was completed in 1942. It is seen here at Bressingham Steam Museum shortly after being rescued for preservation.   8.10.71

(Opposite, top) This Avonside 0-4-0ST, no. 1978 of 1928, was supplied new to the South Western Gas Board, formerly the Bath Gas Company. During the fifties it worked alongside a Peckett built in 1912. Both engines were constructed in Bristol.
31.5.55

(Opposite, bottom) The end of the line for Sentinel 4WTG no. 9615 of 1956 at Cohens' scrapyard, Kettering. *Phyllis* was the only Sentinel owned by the Oxfordshire Ironstone Company. It had a short working life and was just nine years old when this picture was taken.
3.10.65

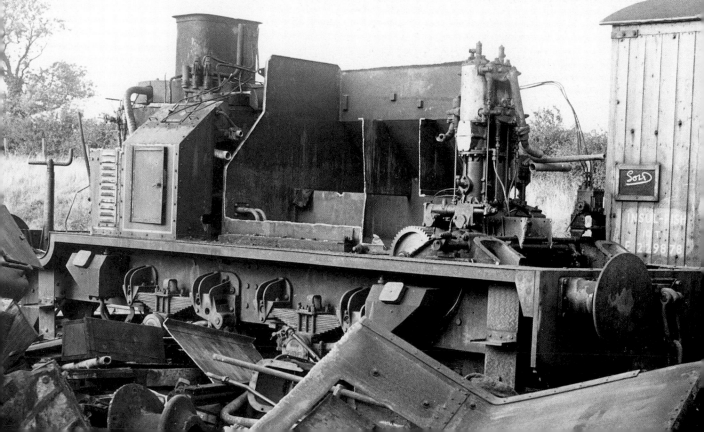

Identification of industrial locomotives can be difficult once all the plates have been removed, but if you are lucky you might find a number stamped on the motion. This is thought to be Peckett no. 1894 *Grace*, built in 1936. It came to Cohens' scrapyard from the Oxfordshire Ironstone Company.   3.10.65

(Opposite, top) Aveling & Porter were better known for road steam vehicles, especially steamrollers, but they did construct a number of railway locomotives. Works no. 9449 was built in 1926. It was basically a road steam design modified for railway use. It is seen here preserved.   July 1995

(Opposite, bottom) Aveling & Porter *Sir Vincent*, no. 8800 of 1917, was supplied new to Vickers-Armstrong of Erith Works, Kent. In 1931 it passed to the British Oil & Cake Mills, also at Erith. The famous Aveling & Porter emblem can be seen on the smokebox door. The engine is superbly restored to working order.   10. 7. 93

Built in 1902 by Andrew Barclay, this locomotive, works no. 880, spent its working life not far away from where it was built for Messrs Glenfield & Kennedy of Kilmarnock.
                                                July 1977

At one time it was thought that this Beyer Garratt locomotive, works no. 6841 of 1937, which spent its working life at the National Coal Board, Baddesley, would be preserved in Canada. Fortunately this did not happen and *William Francis* is seen here on display at Bressingham. 1971

2. All the Sixes – Standard Gauge

Locomotives of the six-coupled wheel arrangement were by far the most numerous in industrial service. They varied considerably in their power output. The postwar 0–6–0STs, for example, which were built by several of the leading companies, were capable of handling very heavy loads. Engines of this type became very popular with the National Coal Board and Stewart & Lloyds Minerals. The working life of industrial engines was long; it was by no means unusual to find examples built in the 1870s and 1880s still at work in the 1950s and 1960s. To keep them running, spare parts would be found from withdrawn engines. As a result derelict hulks could often be seen, as no one was in a hurry to see them cut up.

Withdrawals of main line steam locomotives during the 1960s resulted in a number of ex-Great Western pannier tank engines being purchased by the NCB. Most were of the 57XX design, but there were also three examples of the 15XX class. All of the latter were built in 1949 and worked for the NCB at Coventry.

62

The majority of industrial
locomotives were saddle
tank designs. *Ajax* was an
0–6–0T built by Andrew
Barclay. Originally no. 1605
of 1918, it is seen here at
Stewart & Lloyds, Harlaxton.
At one time this engine was
owned by the Anglo-Persian
Oil Company, being sold to
the Stanton Ironworks
Company in 1940. Stanton
subsequently became part of
the Stewart & Lloyds group.
4.6.66

Most of the locomotives at the giant Stewart & Lloyds Iron & Steel Works were saddle tank designs but no. 17 was an exception. This engine was built by Hudswell Clarke & Company as works no. 1595 and was officially recorded as being built in 1936 – but it was in fact constructed ten years earlier.   12.11.55

(*Opposite, top*) Two Andrew Barclay side-tank engines were to be found at Stewart & Lloyds, Harlaxton. No. 2107 was built in 1941 and supplied new. Officially known as *Harlaxton*, it carried no nameplates when this picture was taken of it standing alongside the coaling bay.   4.6.66

(*Opposite, bottom*) Ridham Dock was in an exposed location, which must have presented problems for the enginemen when the wind was in the wrong direction. *Pioneer II* was built in Kent in 1910. It passed into private ownership in 1967 and afterwards was still to be found at work in that county.   10.7.67

The British Sugar Corporation Peterborough hired this J67/1 no. 68496 from British Railways in 1954 as additional motive power for the peak season. The equipment on the running plate appears to be a generator connected to an aerial in front of the chimney.   4.12.54

One engine that was to become especially well known, particularly by children, was Hudswell Clarke no. 1800 of 1947, owned by the British Sugar Corporation. In preservation it became *Thomas*.
          4.12.54

Manning Wardle locomotives were highly regarded by Stewart & Lloyds. Manning Wardle had shut down in 1926, being taken over by Kitson, but in 1938 they also closed, with all the patterns and goodwill passing to Robert Stephenson & Hawthorns, who subsequently built five locomotives similar to the Manning Wardle design. No. 51 was built in 1940 by Robert Stephenson & Hawthorns as works no. 7003 and was supplied new to Stewart & Lloyds of Corby. In due course it was transferred to the minerals group working in the Corby area and eventually went on to Market Overton. When these pictures were taken it was at Buckminster.   4.6.66

The name *Cranford* was transferred to Avonside no. 1919 of 1924, having previously been carried by an earlier locomotive built by the same company. The engine is seen here returning from the interchange with the former Midland line that was used to forward the ironstone. 23.3.67

It was by no means unusual to find withdrawn locomotives dumped in a siding and robbed of parts to keep others in service. Samuel Williams no. 9, Manning Wardle no. 1617 of 1903, has lost its middle set of driving wheels and coupling rods, together with other parts. Its plates had also been removed. This engine was sold for scrap the following year.

24.5.56

(*Opposite, top*) The British Sugar Corporation at Wissington had two Manning Wardle 0–6–0STs. Due to the seasonal nature of the crop their work was usually concentrated at certain times of the year. *Newcastle*, no. 1532 of 1901, arrived at Wissington from the Spalding factory in 1952, having previously worked at South Lynn and before that for a Wolverhampton-based contractor. The engine is fitted with a spark arrester and the cab is sealed off, as it would not be in steam again until the autumn.

8.5.54

(*Opposite, bottom*) Manning Wardle no. 2006 of 1921 is seen here by the water tank after completing the winter programme at the Wissington sugar factory. It was unlikely to see any further use until the autumn when the next crop would be ready for processing.

8.5.54

This Samuel Williams veteran, Manning Wardle no. 641 of 1877, has many interesting features, including wooden buffers, a small saddle tank and a polished safety valve cover. When this picture was taken few people would have believed that it would still be around in the twenty-first century – especially as it was seventy-nine years old at the time. Happily when steam finished at Samuel Williams, the engine was preserved on site. After a spell at Bressingham Steam Museum it is now at the Bluebell Railway.   24.5.56

(Above) After *No. 4* left Dagenham it was on display at Bressingham where this picture was taken. The very limited protection for the enginemen can be clearly seen .   12.6.73

(Below) The enginemen employed by Samuel Williams kept their engines in first-class external condition. This company preferred the engines built by the highly respected company Manning Wardle, and before 1939 almost its entire fleet was made up of locomotives from this Leeds-based builder. On this tidy engine the number 1 is just visible below the company's name. This was the second no. 1. Although still serviceable, it and the engine behind were out of use at the time. Built in 1903 by Manning Wardle as works no. 1590, no. 1 arrived in March 1934 from H. Arnold & Son, a Doncaster contractor.   24.5.56

Two of Stewart & Lloyds fleet, no. 45 *Colwyn* and no. 48 *Criggion*, were built by Kitsons of Leeds in 1933 and 1936 respectively to a well-tried Manning Wardle design. Kitsons closed in 1938. 22.5.55

(Opposite, top) In a typical location for industrial engines, this is no. 3 *Edgware*, Manning Wardle no. 2045 of 1926, which arrived from C.J. Wills of Edgware, who presumably named the engine. Note the interesting steam crane also in the siding. 24.5.56

(Opposite, bottom) Manning Wardle no. 7. no. 1488 of 1900, fills its tank at the end of the day. The majority of the Samuel Williams steam fleet were purchased second-hand, in this case from Davies, Middleton & Davies of Caerphilly in South Wales in 1929. 24.5.56

Resplendent in its dark green livery Manning Wardle no. 41 *Rhyl* awaits its next turn of duty. Originally works no. 2009, this engine was built in 1921, just five years before the company closed in 1926. In all, Manning Wardle built over two thousand locomotives. Kitsons took over the goodwill, and produced twenty-three engines to Manning Wardle designs.   22.5.55

Stewart & Lloyds of Corby's no. 32 runs through the yard with a match truck. This sturdy outside cylinder 0–6–0ST locomotive was built by Hawthorn, Leslie & Company as works no. 3888 in 1936.
12.11.55

The Stewart & Lloyds locomotives all carried running numbers. No. 7, Andrew Barclay no. 1268 of 1912, arrived at Corby from the Clydesdale works in 1934. It is seen here hauling a train of slag wagons, with a match truck between them and the engine.
12.11.55

No. 6 of the Stewart & Lloyds fleet was Andrew Barclay works no. 1241 of 1911, seen here taking on coal supplies from a wagon thoughtfully positioned in the works yard. This engine was supplied new and previously carried the name *Ironworks No.2*. A well aimed shovel-full of coal can be seen on its way to the engine.   12.11.55

The movement of slag was an important and continuous requirement at iron and steel works. The very hot waste material was transported in special wagons. Locomotive no. 21, built by Hawthorn Leslie & Company as works no. 3931 in 1938, is seen here at Stewart & Lloyds of Corby.   12.11.55

Immaculate in its mid-green livery, this is Hudswell Clarke no. 39 *Rhos*, no. 1308 of 1918. Prior to 1949 this engine worked at the steel works. In 1955 *Rhos* was the only member of the fleet to have outside cylinders (although a small Hunslet of this type was scrapped in 1953). The Stewart & Lloyds mineral engines covered considerable distances as the Corby system comprised almost 40 miles of track. It was the most extensive ironstone railway in the British Isles.

22.5.55

One of the most interesting engines at the Stewart & Lloyds Steelworks at Corby was no. 25, a sturdy 0–6–0ST built by the Yorkshire Engine Company in Sheffield as works no. 327 in 1882. Unusual features include the saddle tank shape, the extra tall chimney and the solid wheels.   12.11.55

(*Opposite*) Only two 0–6–0STs were to be found in the sizeable locomotive stud at Wellingborough Ironworks. Peckett no. 1235 of 1910 *Forward* was one of them; the other was an Andrew Barclay. This engine arrived from Stanton Ironworks in the mid-1930s and spent some time working at a local quarry. All the other engines at Wellingborough were 0–4–0STs.

11.11.55

(*Overleaf*) The massive steelworks at Corby required a large stud of locomotives to carry out all the necessary movements in and out of the works. This is no. 40, Hawthorn & Leslie no. 3375 of 1919, pictured in a typical setting and with a good head of steam. No. 40 arrived at Corby in 1931 from the North Lincs Iron Company.

Stewart & Lloyds No. 38 *Dolobran* worked for many years at the steelworks before transferring to the minerals division. Constructed by Manning Wardle of Leeds in 1910 as works no. 1762, it was typical of the well-built locomotives supplied by the company.   22.5.55

Under repair in the back of the shed at Stewart & Lloyds of Corby was no. 10 *Treasurer*, built by Hunslet of Leeds in 1929 as works no. 1446. This engine was purchased from the Oxfordshire Ironstone Company in 1937.   12.11.55

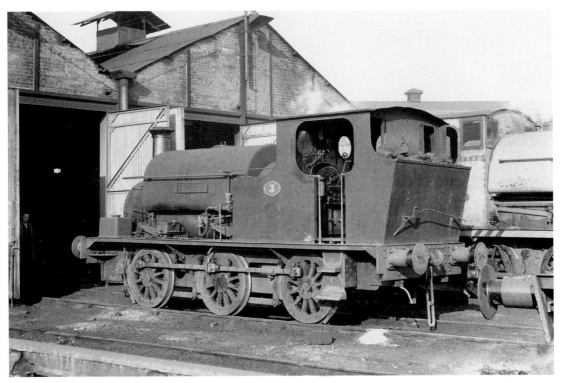

Another of the Corby 0–6–0STs, no. 3 carried the name *Pen Green*. It was supplied new in 1903 by Hudswell Clarke as works no. 607. Locomotives at the works were built by a number of different engine builders.   12.11.55

Corby no. 9 was built by Hudswell Clarke in 1919 as works no. 1383 and was supplied new to the company, at one time being named *Ironworks 3*. The plate on the saddle tank was presumably where the nameplate was fitted.   12.11.55

The locomotives at Samuel Williams, Dagenham were kept in good external condition, as can be seen by this picture of no. 15. Hudswell Clarke no. 1676 of 1937 was one of several engines to arrive in 1940.   24.5.56

Hudswell Clarke no. 1526 worked at Samuel Williams for seventeen years. Built in 1924, it came from McAlpine in 1940. It carried the number 10 and was painted in blue livery. Behind it is the veteran Manning Wardle no. 641 of 1877, carrying the number 4.   24.5.56

Hudswell Clarke & Company of Railway Foundry were one of several companies based in Leeds. Samuel Williams no. 15 was Hudswell Clarke works no. 1676 of 1937, and was typical of many built by the company for industrial use. No. 15 was purchased from McAlpine in 1940.   24.5.56

At one time carrying the name *Ironworks No. 1*, Stewart & Lloyds of Corby's no. 5, Andrew Barclay 0–6–0ST no. 1241 of 1911, was supplied new. Two consecutively numbered Andrew Barclay locomotives were built for the company in 1911.   12.11.55

Resplendent in its bright yellow livery, this is Corby no. 11, Hawthorn Leslie no. 3824 built in 1934. This was the first of eleven 0–6–0STs supplied new to Stewart & Lloyds in the 1930s. 12.11.55

This sturdy Bagnall 0–6–0ST *Cranford No. 2*, works no. 2668, was supplied new in 1942 to the Cranford Ironstone Quarries. It is seen here at the small shed, its days work over.   6.5.65

The line from the Cranford quarries ran under the Huntingdon – Kettering road to the area where ore was loaded on to British Railways wagons which then eventually reached the Midland main line. *Cranford No. 2* Bagnall no. 2668 of 1942 is seen busy shunting.   16.5.65

(Opposite, top) Time was running out for *Cranford*, Avonside works no. 1918 of 1923, as within a short time it was to be withdrawn. Note the improvised chimney and the sheet at the back of the cab to give protection to the enginemen. Note the chimney repairs.   9.5.65

(Opposite, bottom) Less than a year later *Cranford* was derelict. All its plates had been removed. This engine had been supplied new when the quarry system was converted from metre to standard gauge. It had a long working life but would not have been very popular with the crews as it did not have an all-over cab.   17.3.66

Hudswell Clarke no. 1579 of 1926 arrived at Cranford ironstone quarries in 1957. Two engines were normally in operation here, making a fine sight as they hauled heavy loads from the quarry.   9.5.65

(Opposite, top) Avonside no. 1945 of 1926 was supplied new to the Central Sugar Company (which later became British Sugar). It is seen here shunting at Peterborough during the peak of the 1954 season.   4.12.54

(Opposite, bottom) This powerful 0–6–0ST was built by Hudswell Clarke & Company in 1955 as works no. 1881. It was photographed outside the shed at Park Hall colliery. The National Coal Board owned a large number of locomotives which were distributed between the considerable number of collieries still operating in the mid-1960s.   20.3.66

Typical of the many postwar 0–6–0STs built by Hunslet of Leeds, works no. 3836 of 1955 carried the number S116 and was to be found at the National Coal Board's Primrose Hill Colliery.   25.3.66

(Opposite, top) The Port of Bristol Authority at Avonmouth purchased locomotives new from Pecketts of Bristol over many years. Two were bought in 1934; one of these was *Westbury*, works no. 1877, seen here against a typical dock background.   8.9.56

(Opposite, bottom) Peckett works no. 1377 *Edward*, built in 1914, had been withdrawn from service at Avonmouth Docks two years before this picture was taken. It had spent most of this time in a siding but seems to be complete except for the missing front and back buffers.   8.9.56

The driver of *Clifton*, Peckett works no. 2037 of 1943, was pleased to stop his engine for this photograph to be taken at Avonmouth Docks. The Port of Bristol Authority owned the extensive docks. 8.9.56

(Opposite, top) The oldest Peckett still to be found at Avonmouth Docks in 1956 was works no. 808 *Kenneth*, built at Bristol in 1900. This engine had a shaped dome and Salter safety valves. 8.9.56

(Opposite, bottom) The last of the Avonside engines to arrive at Avonmouth Docks was works no. 1800 *Percy*, built in 1918. All the locomotives here were 0–6–0STs, although a solitary 0–4–0ST had been in use at the docks for a short period. 8.9.56

At the time of my visit seven 0–6–0ST locomotives built by the Avonside Engine Company of Bristol were in service at Avonmouth Docks. *Alfred*, works no. 1679 of 1914, had just arrived back on shed.   8.9.56

(Opposite, top) Most of the engines at Avonmouth stood outside. Here a work-stained Peckett *Henbury*, works no. 1940 of 1937, stands ready for its next turn of duty shunting on the docks.   8.9.56

(Opposite, bottom) The last of the engines built by Pecketts to arrive at Avonmouth Docks was *Redland*, works no. 2038 of 1943. Four identical locomotives with consecutive numbers were supplied to the docks that year.   8.9.56

Another of the Stewart & Lloyd engines in yellow livery was no. 15, built by Hawthorns in 1934 as works no. 3836. Locomotives were to be found in many places throughout the massive complex. At night the glow in the sky from the furnaces could be seen for miles around.   12.11.55

(*Opposite, top*) Its day's work done, Stewart & Lloyd no. 28 *Beaumont*, Hawthorn & Leslie works no. 2469 of 1900, heads through the Corby Steelworks complex en route to the locomotive shed. This engine arrived in 1945 from the North Walbottle Coal Company. When this picture was taken it had just three more years left in service.   12.11.55

(*Opposite, bottom*) The locomotive stud at Stewart & Lloyds of Corby included representatives of several major engine builders, but only one example built by Pecketts of Bristol was present in the mid-fifties. This was no. 8 *Margot*, works no. P1456 built in 1918. Previously at Islip Ironworks near Thrapston, this engine moved to Corby in May 1950. Islip Ironworks closed in 1943, but the quarries there remained open until 1952.   12.11.55

No. 6, Andrew Barclay no. 1497 of 1916, brings up a train of three loaded ore wagons from the quarry. This engine was owned by the South Durham Steel & Iron Company. It is seen here at Irchester but it had also worked at Storefield after transferring from the company's Malleable Works in Stockton in 1954. Before coming into South Durham ownership it had worked in a colliery.   30.8.67

(*Opposite, top*) This spare boiler stood on a flat wagon at the Nassington Ironstone Quarries. Behind it is the Peckett *Buccleuch*, no. 1232 of 1910, which had stood out of use for some considerable time. Originally supplied new to Glendon East Quarries, *Buccleuch* enjoyed a long working life, seeing use at Market Overton and Harlaxton among other sites. It ended its days at Nassington.   19.3.67

(*Opposite, bottom*) Having been dismantled, Avonside no. 1787 of 1917 probably was found to be beyond economical repair, or was simply withdrawn to be used for spares. Whichever, it was in a sorry state in the derelict line at the South Durham Steel & Iron Company at Irchester.   20.1.66

Another of the engines working for Stewart & Lloyds at Glendon was no. 50 *Carmarthen*, built by Kitsons as works no. 5478 in 1936 to the basic Manning Wardle design. Kitsons had taken over from Manning Wardle when it closed in 1926.

20.4.67

(Opposite) The Stewart & Lloyds Minerals Ltd locomotives were painted in a dark green livery, which made them easily recognisable as they moved between the company's several locations in Northamptonshire. No. 49 *Caerphilly* was built to a Manning Wardle design by Kitson & Company of the Airedale Foundry, Leeds and supplied new to Stewart & Lloyds of Corby before transferring to the Minerals group. Works no. 5477 built in 1936, it is seen here shunting at Glendon. Next to it is a typical steel-bodied 27-ton Tippler wagon.

30.3.67

(Opposite) Stewart & Lloyds Minerals Ltd operated a very extensive system of ironstone tramways in the Corby area. A rail tour was organised on Saturday 22 May 1955 with veteran Manning Wardle no. 35, built in 1895 as works no. 317, providing the motive power. The 'special' train is seen here at Oakley sidings, the first call on the tour. At one time this engine carried the name *Rhiwnant*. It arrived at Corby via a contractor, having previously worked at Rhyader in the ownership of Birmingham Corporation Waterworks.   22.5.55

(Right) The massive dragline at Oakley dwarfs the Manning Wardle and its train. At the time this giant machine was thought to be the largest in the world. Careful study of the picture reveals just how much topsoil had to be removed to gain access to the thick bed of ironstone.

22.5.55

(Below) The rail tour took in Oakley Cowthick and Gretton Brook, before heading north to Harringworth and Wakerley. The railway, comprising 40 miles of track, supplied iron ore to the works.

22.5.55

The rail tour over, the veteran Manning Wardle was photographed back at Gretton Brook shortly before returning to the locomotive shed to await its next duties. The following year this engine spent a short time working at Glendon quarries.
22.5.55

(Opposite) Members of the rail tour re-boarding the platelayers' vans for the next leg of the journey. These vans were important pieces of equipment which played a vital role in maintaining the extensive rail systems operated from Corby.
22.5.55

Just twelve years old when this picture was taken, *Rutland* was the youngest engine present at Stewart & Lloyds of Harlaxton. Built by Andrew Barclay in 1954 as works no. 2351, it was supplied new. During its life it worked on several different Stewart & Lloyd quarry lines.   4.6.66

(Opposite, top) The Nassington Ironstone Quarries operated two Hunslet 0–6–0STs, both of which were supplied new. *Ring Haw* no. 1982 of 1940 was one of them. Nassington was one of the last ironstone quarries to operate steam locomotives.   19.3.67

(Opposite, bottom) Hunslet 0–6–0ST *Jacks Green*, built in 1939 as works no. 1953, was the other of the two identical locomotives supplied to the Nassington Quarries. Both these engines have survived into preservation.   19.3.67

This 0–6–0ST, *Bickershaw*, was built by Hunslets of Leeds in 1933. It is seen here at Park Hall Colliery after being withdrawn to await scrapping. Note the unusual chimney which is certainly not one of the usual Hunslet pattern.   20.3.66

Hunslets of Leeds produced considerable numbers of this type of 0–6–0ST over a long period. *Jubilee* no. 1725 was built in 1935. It is seen here at Newmarket Silkstone Colliery, part of the National Coal Board's no. 8 Castleford Area.   20.3.66

Hunslet no. 1660 of 1930 about to be cut up at Cashmores' Newport scrapyard. This engine was owned by the Admiralty at Caerwent in its working days. This was the only industrial locomotive present at Cashmores at the time of my visit; all the others were British Railways engines of various classes.   25.10.65

A typical example of the stud of modern 0–6–0STs operated by Stewart & Lloyds Minerals at Corby, no. 57 was built by Robert Stephenson & Hawthorns as no. 7668 in 1950. It was one of a batch supplied new to the company in that same year, joining a number of other locomotives built by Stephenson & Hawthorns in the early 1940s.   22.5.55

No. 45 *Colwyn*,
Kitson works no.
5473, was originally
supplied new to the
Stewart & Lloyds
steelworks in 1934.
It was transferred
with a number of
other engines to the
minerals operation
in 1949.   22.5.55

The facilities available for the maintenance of industrial locomotives varied considerably. Stewart & Lloyds of Harlaxton was home for a number of engines. Here Andrew Barclay 0-6-0T *Ajax*, no. 1605 of 1918, stands over the pit, with a water crane in the background.   4.6.66

(Opposite, top) Several of the Oxfordshire Ironstone Company's engines ended their days at Cohens' scrapyard, Kettering. Peckett no.1981 *John* was built at Bristol in 1941. When this picture was taken it was one of three Oxfordshire Ironstone engines present.   3.10.65

(Opposite, bottom) Stewart & Lloyds Minerals Ltd, No. 51 seen here in poor external condition and stored out of use at Harlaxton. Built in 1940 by Robert Stephenson & Hawthorn as works no. 7003, it was basically a copy of a much earlier Manning Wardle design.   4.6.66

R&W Hawthorn, Leslie & Company's Forth Bank Works were to be found at Newcastle upon Tyne. This company built many locomotives for industrial use. No. 3892 of 1936 was supplied new to Irchester Quarries, which later became part of the South Durham Steel & Iron Company.   30.1.66

Manning Wardle & Company were located at The Boyne Engine Works, Hunslet, Leeds. Also in that district were Kitson & Company, Hudswell Clarke & Company and the Hunslet Engine Company. Manning Wardle had a good reputation for well-built locomotives. The works plate in this picture was photographed on 0–6–0ST no. 1532 *Newcastle* of 1910, owned by the British Sugar Corporation.

8.5.54

3. Other Gauges

In the 1950s one of the largest concentrations of narrow-gauge steam locomotives was to be found in the North Wales slate quarries. The majority of these engines were built by Hunslets of Leeds, but by no means all; other well-known companies also built a few examples. These included De Winton of Caernarvon, who supplied vertical boiler 0–4–0Ts to several companies from the 1870s onwards. Most had long been scrapped by the 1950s, but fortunately a few examples still survived.

Most of the slate quarry systems were 1ft 11½in gauge, but there were small variations, such as the Dinorwic track being at 1ft 10¾in. The Penmaenmawr and Welsh Granite Company used a 3ft track gauge. At one time this company also operated De Winton vertical boiler locomotives, but all were out of use or already scrapped by 1950. One of the derelicts, *Watkin*, built in 1893, stood out for many years slowly rusting away. Exposure to the salt-laden atmosphere here soon took its toll. The Dinorwic slate quarries operated a fleet of narrow-gauge engines as well as three Hunslets 4ft gauge to work the main line, conveying slate to the port installation from where it was dispatched by sea or rail.

It was not only in North Wales that you could find narrow-gauge systems. One fascinating line of 1ft 11½in gauge was to be found at the Southam Works of the Rugby Portland Cement Company. Here were to be found six neat 0–6–0STs built by Peckett & Sons of Bristol and all supplied new between 1903 and 1923. At Kettering the quarry line was a 3ft system, operated by the Kettering Iron & Coal Company. The principal motive power was supplied by 0–6–0STs built by Manning Wardle, together with two 0–4–0STs built by Black, Hawthorn & Company in 1897 and 1885. Not far away at Wellingborough, Stewart & Lloyds operated a 1m-gauge line.

There were many other fascinating narrow-gauge industrial lines to be found at this time. One that was to become widely known was Bowaters' United Kingdom Pulp & Paper Mills at Sittingbourne, Kent. Locomotives built by several different companies operated on the 2ft 6in gauge. Most were fitted with large spark arresters owing to the high fire risk. This, at first glance, made them resemble the engines you would expect to find in a Cuban sugar plantation!

One narrow-gauge line that attracted much attention during the 1950s was the 1ft 11½in system of the Rugby Portland Cement Company at Southam in Warwickshire. Four 0–6–0STs, all named after geological periods, worked this tramway. *Jurassic* was the oldest engine here, built by Pecketts of Bristol in 1903 as works no. 1008. It is seen here in late autumn sunshine passing the locomotive shed with its train of four loaded wagons. This photograph was taken just two years before the tramway was superseded by road transport in October 1956.

24.11.54

This side view of *Triassic*, Peckett no. 1270 of 1911 illustrates clearly the diminutive dimensions of these locomotives. The driving wheels cannot be seen, but the photograph gives some idea of their small diameter. Note also the distinctive tall chimney and large brass works plate.   24.11.54

(Opposite, top) Triassic again, quietly raising steam outside the locomotive shed ready for its next duty. This engine had been rebuilt at Southam three years before this picture was taken.   24.11.54

(Opposite, bottom) Liassic shunting loaded narrow-gauge tipping wagons. All four of the Southam Pecketts survived into preservation.   24.11.54

The youngest of the three Manning Wardles at Kettering was no. 1675 *Kettering Furnaces No. 8*, built in 1906 and supplied new. Unlike its two sisters it had not been rebuilt. Conditions on the day of my visit could not have been worse, with heavy rain. Working to and from the quarry must have been a rough ride for the enginemen, judging by the track in this picture.   11.11.55

(Opposite, top) Piles of ash and clinker lie alongside the track. *Kettering Furnaces no. 6*, works no. 1123 of 1889, stands outside the locomotive shed in steam, ready to work to the quarry.   11.11.55

(Opposite, bottom) Three 3ft-gauge 0–6–0STs built by Manning Wardle of Leeds carried the numbers 6, 7 and 8. Here works no. 1370 *Kettering Furnaces No. 7*, supplied new in 1897, prepares to leave for the quarry. Just five years before this picture was taken, it had been rebuilt by Robert Stephenson & Hawthorns.   11.11.55

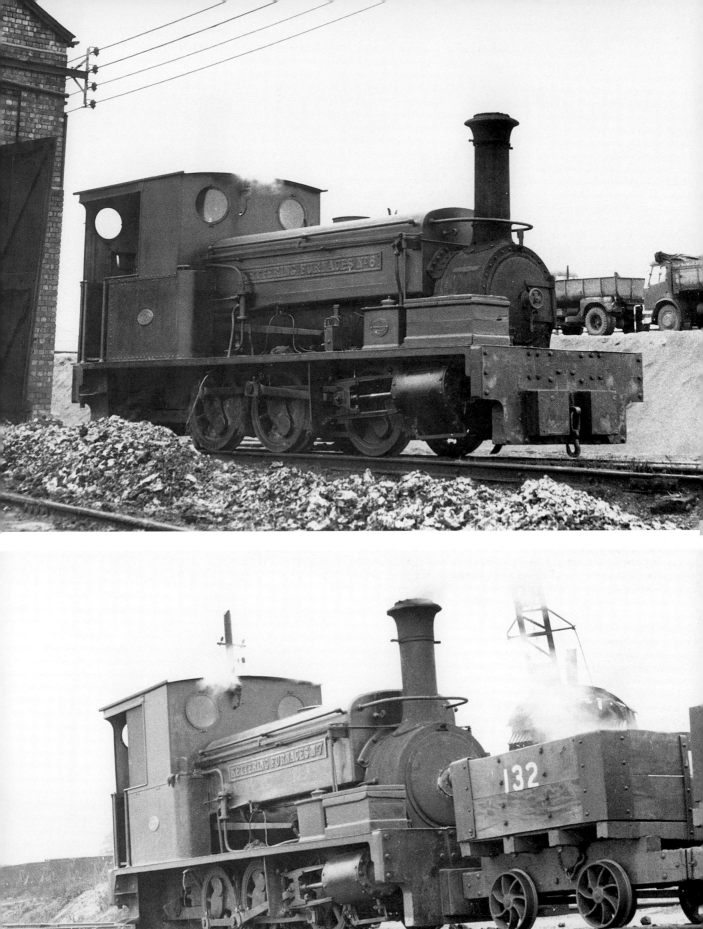

Judging by the layer of dust that had settled on Dinorwic's *Cackler*, Hunslet no. 671 of 1898, it had been some considerable time since it was last used. This engine formerly carried the name *Port Dinorwic*. It had a 4ft 6in wheelbase and was one of only two engines in the 'Mills' class. 16.7.64

(Opposite, top) Three of these diminutive Black Hawthorn & Company 3ft-gauge 0–4–0STs were supplied to the Kettering Iron & Coal Company. The first, no. 501, built in 1879, was followed six years later by the second engine, and two years later by the third. The original locomotive carried the name *Kettering Furnaces No. 2*, which only just fitted on the saddle tank. Little was provided in the way of protection for its driver, who shared the footplate with a supply of coal. 11.11.56

(Opposite, bottom) Manning Wardle no. 1123 *Kettering Furnaces No. 6* was built in 1889 and was supplied to the company via a contractor based in Nottinghamshire, where it had carried the name *Union Jack*. Robert Stephenson & Hawthorns had rebuilt the engine in 1949. 11.11.55

(Overleaf) The Dinorwic 'Alice' class locomotives had domeless boilers, and most were built without cabs. Their short 3ft 3in wheelbase enabled them to cope with tight curves, while their wheel diameter was just 1ft 8in. *George B*, works no. 680, was built at Leeds in 1898 and is seen here passing an old quarry face. It was supplied new to the company and by the time this picture was taken it had already completed sixty-six years' service. Its driver was obviously keen to maintain its fine external condition. 16.7.64

There were three locomotives in the Dinorwic 'Port' class, all built with cabs. *Dolbadarn* (formerly no. 2) was built in 1922 as works no. 1430. Note the wagon used as a tender. There was little room for the driver as coal and chains took up the far side of the footplate. As did all the Welsh slate quarries, the Dinorwic built up huge piles of waste slate.   16.7.64

Hunslet no. 589 *Blanche*, built in 1893, receives attention in the works of the Penrhyn slate quarries, Bethesda. Three engines of this type, known as the Penrhyn 'Main Line' class, were used to transport slate to the coast for onward transportation by sea or rail. *Blanche* and sister engine *Linda*, both built in 1893, were purchased by the Ffestiniog Railway, while the third, *Charles*, built in 1882, became a museum exhibit.   12.6.63

Avonside no. 2067 *Marchlyn* of 1933 was supplied new to the Durham Water Board and was used in the construction of Burnhope reservoir at Wearhead, carrying the name *Wear*. In 1936 it was sold to the Penrhyn slate quarries. Note the typical slate wagon and the small tender attached to the engine.
12.6.63

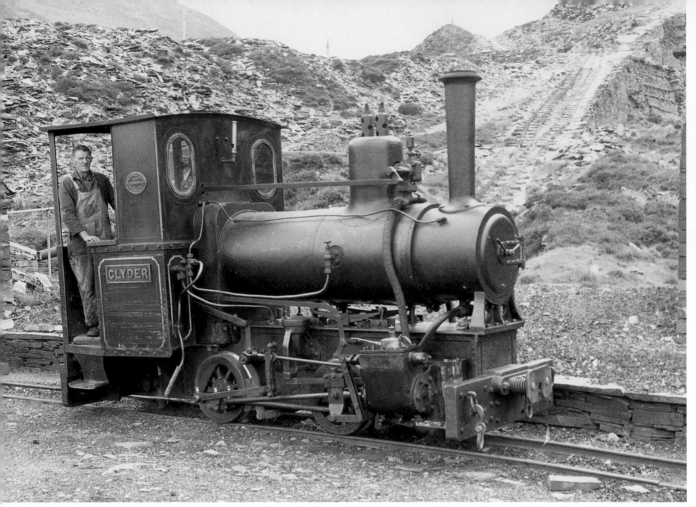

Shunting on the lower level at Penrhyn on one of my visits was Andrew Barclay *Glyder*, no. 1994 of 1931. This engine was one of five purchased from the Durham Water Board between 1934 and 1938. In the background is one of the inclines and several huge waste tips.   25.6.62

(Opposite, top) This Hunslet was one of four delivered new to the Penrhyn slate quarries in the 1880s. *Winifred*, works no. 364 of 1885, had already clocked up a remarkable seventy-seven years' service. This engine was one of three belonging to the 'Port' class.   25.6.62

(Opposite, bottom) Many years had passed since this De Winton vertical boiler locomotive had been used. Built in 1877 at nearby Caernarvon, it was in a sorry state; numerous parts had been removed, including the coupling rods. As with all the Penrhyn derelicts, it somehow survived into preservation.   25.6.62

Orenstein & Koppel A.G. of Berlin built this 0–4–0WT in 1912 as works no. 5668 *Eigiau*. It arrived at the Penrhyn slate quarries from Dolgarrog Reservoir in 1929. Its working days over, it joined the other derelicts and began to slowly rust away. It was eventually rescued and returned to running order.   25.6.62

(Opposite, top) Fireless locomotives were used in locations where a high fire risk existed, and two engines of this type were in the stock of Bowaters' at Sittingbourne. Here *Unique*, built by Bagnall in 1923 as works no. 2216, shunts in the yard. The Bowaters rail system was 2ft 6in gauge.   10.7.67

(Opposite, bottom) At first glance this picture could easily be taken for a railway scene in a distant country. The large spark arrester fitted to Bowaters' Bagnall no. 2472 *Alpha*, built in 1932, was very important because of the fire risk but looked very strange to those accustomed to British industrial locomotives.   10.7.67

Lying out of use in a siding at Bowaters was Kerr Stuart 0–4–2ST no. 1049 of 1908, *Excelsior*. Judging by its condition, it would appear not to have worked for some time.   10.7.67

Locomotive overhaul, repairs and maintenance were carried out in the Bowaters Company workshops. Here one of the oldest engines, Kerr Stuart 0–4–2ST *Leader* of 1905, receives attention. This engine and its sister *Premier*, also built in 1905, were rebuilt in 1912.   10.7.67

Bowaters' Bagnall *Conqueror*, works no. 2192, was built at Stafford in 1922. It is seen here with coaching stock. Note the three large oil cans on the running plate. All the engines carried these in varying positions. 10.7.67

0–6–2T *Chevallier*, works no. 1877, was built by Manning Wardle in 1915. It was purchased by Bowaters from the Admiralty in 1950, having previously worked on the Chattenden & Upnor Railway. 10.7.67

Four 0–4–2STs built by Kerr Stuart were operated by Bowaters of Sittingbourne. *Melior*, no. 4219 of 1924, was the youngest. It is seen here outside the locomotive shed ready for its next tour of duty.

10.7.67

Bagnalls of Stafford built 0–6–2T *Triumph* in 1934 as works no. 2511. This engine was fitted with an unattractive spark arrester, as were most of the locomotives working on the Bowaters' 2ft 6in system.

10.7.67

The Hunslet Engine Company built this 1m-gauge 0–4–0ST in 1888 as works no. 473. It was supplied new to Wellingborough Ironstone Quarries, becoming their no. 4. It stood dumped in a siding for a considerable time before being scrapped in October 1959. 11.11.55

The Stewart & Lloyds' locomotives at Wellingborough were fitted with spark arresters because the line ran adjacent to agricultural land. No. 86, Peckett no. 1871 of 1934, is seen here outside the locomotive shed, with some typical ironstone wagons in the background. 1.10.88

Metre-gauge rail systems are commonplace in many continental countries. One was to be found at Wellingborough, which had several owners before being taken over by Stewart & Lloyds Minerals Ltd. At this point all three of the Pecketts were painted green and numbered into their series.   1.10.66

In 1931 Pecketts of Bristol supplied two metre-gauge 0–6–0STs to the Wellingborough Iron Company which later became part of the Stewart & Lloyds group. No. 86 was one of them.   1.10.66

Anyone on the Wellingborough – Finedon road must have looked in amazement as the rail tour crossed the road. The locomotives and wagons would have been familiar, but this time they were loaded with people! Here Peckett no. 87, works no. 2029 of 1942, banks the train. 17.6.64

In 1964 Stewart & Lloyds Minerals Ltd kindly gave permission for a rail tour of the Wellingborough system. As nothing other than the ironstone wagons were available everyone scrambled into these. No. 85, Peckett no. 1870 of 1934, is seen here heading the train, with no. 87, Peckett no. 2029 of 1942, at the rear. 17.6.64

The Scottish Gas Board's large rail installation at Granton Gas Works in Edinburgh also included a 2ft 6in gauge line. One of the engines used here was Andrew Barclay no. 1954, built in 1928, which is seen here under repair, minus wheels and supported by wooden blocks. It had been like this for some time.   22.8.55

Locomotives built by Andrew Barclay, Sons & Company at the Caledonia Works in Kilmarnock were highly regarded by private companies and state-owned companies alike This works plate was fitted to a 2ft 6in gauge locomotive at Granton Works in Edinburgh.   22.8.55

The Penmaenmawr & Welsh Granite Company at one time operated a number of De Winton vertical boiler locomotives on the 3ft-gauge line. By the late 1940s those that remained were derelict. *Watkin* was built at Caernarvon in 1893. By the early 1960s years of exposure to the salt-laden atmosphere had taken its toll; surprisingly it was still remarkably intact, although the brake gear and coupling rods had long since been removed.   July 1961

Three of these 0–6–0Ts were supplied new to the Dinorwic slate quarries to work the 4ft line to the coast where slate was dispatched by sea and rail. This was known as the Padarn Railway. One of the three had already been cut up when this picture of *Amathaea* and *Velinheli* was taken at a spot known as Gilfach Ddu. 16.7.64

(Opposite, top) Typical of French industrial steam locomotives, this is the metre-gauge Corpet 0-6-0T no. 493 *Cambrai*. Built in 1888, it arrived in England in 1936 from Chemin de fer du Cambreisi and was in the locomotive stud operated by Loddington Ironstone Quarries, Northamptonshire. July 1961

(Opposite, bottom) *Cambrai* on display at the Tywyn Narrow-Gauge Museum. The engine had a sizeable cab, with large look-out windows at the front and much smaller ones at the back. July 1961

Bagnall locomotive no. 2043 of 1917 *Kidbrooke* was withdrawn from service in 1941 by its owners, the Oakeley Slate Quarries Company of Blaenau Ffestiniog. It became derelict and was left out for well over fifty years. It has now been restored to full working order.
27.5.2000

When I visited the Penrhyn slate quarries in 1962 Orenstein & Koppel no. 5668, *Eigiau*, built in 1912, was in the derelict line and I never thought I would see it in action again. But here it is at work once more at Bressingham Steam Museum.   Early 1970s